Dane Love is the author of numerous books on Scotland in general and on Ayrshire in particular. He was born in Cumnock but lives in the countryside near Auchinleck. He is descended from Robin Love, who fought for Bonnie Prince Charlie at the battles of Prestonpans and Culloden. A member of Ayrshire Archaeological and Natural History Society, he is also the Honorary Secretary of the Scottish Covenanter Memorials Association and a Fellow of the Society of Antiquaries of Scotland. For much of his life he worked as a teacher at Irvine Royal Academy. He enjoys travelling around Scotland with his wife, visiting historic sites and doing research.

Girvan harbour, sketched by Robert Bryden in 1891.

Title Page and Back Cover: Plan of Ayr Harbour in 1772.
Following Page: Girvan Harbour fishing boats.

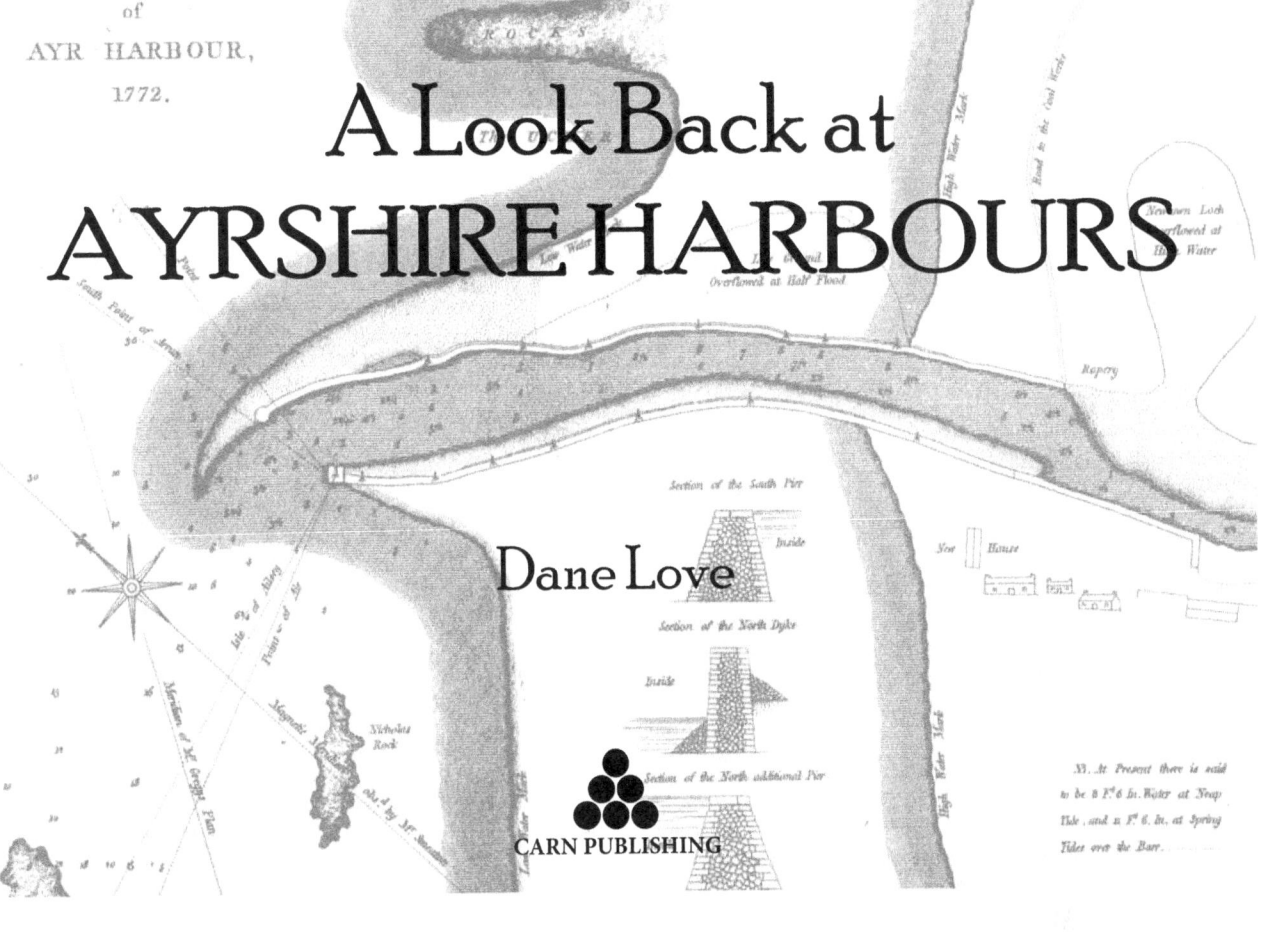

A Look Back at AYRSHIRE HARBOURS

Dane Love

CARN PUBLISHING

© Dane Love, 2024.
First Published in Great Britain, 2024.

ISBN - 978 1 911043 24 9

Published by Carn Publishing Ltd.,
Lochnoran House,
Auchinleck,
Ayrshire, KA18 3JW.

www.carnpublishing.com

Printed by Bell & Bain Ltd.,
Glasgow, G46 7UQ.

The right of the author to be identified as the author of this work has been asserted by him in accordance with the Copyright, Designs and Patents Act, 1988.

All rights reserved. No part of this publication can be reproduced, stored, or transmitted in any form, or by any means, electronic, mechanical or photocopying, recording or otherwise, without the express written permission of the publisher.

Introduction

Ayrshire has its fair share of iconic ports, piers and harbours along its 84-mile coastline. Historically, the small river-mouth harbours of Irvine, Ayr and Girvan were the main ports of the county, and each vied with each other to gain the most trade with Ireland and beyond. Indeed, Irvine became the third largest port in Scotland in the eighteenth century, with much of the trade from Glasgow passing through it. Ayr also claimed to be the third largest port in the country at one time. Politics and wars caused the business at the ports to rise and fall, imports being susceptible to the whims of the period. The importation of port and wine, tobacco and other goods has ended, basics such as timber and grain continuing.

In addition to the estuary ports, small fishing bases existed in coves and sheltered bays, initially with boats hauled up onto shingle beaches. Several small inlets were developed as sheltered spots where a boat could be anchored, or else tied up alongside a stone-built wharf.

Some of these small harbours survive, such as the old harbour at Portencross. Others have long-since gone out of use, such as the tiny harbour at Quarter, between Skelmorlie and Largs. This did not have any great piers or breakwaters, but it did have a few walls built alongside the rocks, creating a basin where small boats could be berthed. No buildings associated with the harbour appear to have existed, but it once had a crane on the north side of the basin, with a track down to it from the public road.

In the early nineteenth century the creation of more substantial basins and protective walls was promoted by several major landowners, in particular the Duke of Portland at Troon and the Earl of Eglinton at Ardrossan. In each case they were developed to service a hinterland that needed to export coal or iron. Both these ports were to be serviced by canals or railways, and though some of the grandiose plans never came to fruition, both ports were commercial successes and continue to operate, though the main purpose of them has changed over the years. Smaller harbours were also developed at this time, such as Ballantrae and Dunure.

The arrival of the pleasure steamer and the growing tourist trade resulted in the creation of piers specifically for the purpose, such as at Portencross and Fairlie, or the adaptation of existing piers and harbours to allow steamers to berth. Steamers on the Firth of Clyde were popular between the 1880s and the start of the First World War, and competition between the different companies that operated them was fierce. Many tales exist of steamers racing each other from port to pier, and not a few accidents or collisions occurred as a result.

The pleasure aspect of the steamer at the pier has gone, apart from the occasion visit of PS *Waverley*, the last sea-going paddle steamer in the world, or the MV *Balmoral*. Nowadays the ferry for Arran or Cumbrae has replaced them to some extent, tourists island-hopping from Largs and Ardrossan, or in some cases Troon. Another growing aspect of the Ayrshire port is the increasing popularity of sailing on the west coast. Yachts and other pleasure boats circumnavigate Arran, Bute and the Cumbraes, their anchorage being in purpose-built marinas, such as Largs at Kelburn, or in adapted harbours with new pontoons, as at Ardrossan and Troon, or to a lesser extent at Ayr, Maidens and Girvan.

Fishing has been an important trade over the years, though has declined considerably in modern times. The herring industry was prolific in the nineteenth century, and there are many accounts of dozens of fishing boats docking in the harbours of the county, landing the 'silver darlings' which could be salted in barrels and kept for the winter. To boost the economy after the two world wars, fishing was promoted, and many new vessels were commissioned. An overfishing resulted in a ban from 1977-1983, with the consequence of many vessels giving up their trade.

General coastal trade has taken place from the traditional harbours, such as Ayr, Irvine and Ardrossan, and in the case of Ayr continues to do so. The harbour was used for sending coal to Ireland, and in recent years has seen a jump in the importation of timber, often just from elsewhere in Scotland. Grain has been imported in quantity to Ayr, as well as components such as towers and blades for wind turbines. Troon continues to import timber.

The construction of boats and ships has occurred at various places along the coast. At the northern end, at Fairlie, William Fife and Son made many successful timber-hulled racing yachts from 1803 until 1939, much prized by their owners, including Sir Thomas Lipton, who commissioned them to make a yacht to participate in the America's Cup. Ardrossan, Irvine, Troon and Ayr had major shipbuilding firms based at the harbour for many years, sadly all gone now. The only ship engineering business of any consequence to survive is Alexander Noble at Girvan, which continues to make timber and steel hulled fishing boats and other vessels.

Ayrshire's harbours and piers are in some cases now owned by private companies, such as Associated British Ports, which owns Ayr and Troon. Ardrossan is the property of Peel Ports Group Ltd, successor to Clydeport, and Irvine is owned by Irvine Harbour Company, part of NPL group. The harbour at Girvan is owned by South Ayrshire Council, but operated by Ayrshire Roads Alliance, as is that at Ballantrae. The pier and harbour at Largs is the property of Caledonian Maritime Assets Ltd. Other harbours may be owned by local authorities, but are operated by local trusts or users, such as Dunure.

This short history and pictorial wander round the old harbours, ports and piers of the county will be of interest to all with a love of the county, whether associated with the sea or not.

Site of Skelmorlie Pier

The village of Skelmorlie was only really established as a place where large bungalows and villas were erected, often owned by businessmen from Greenock, Glasgow and other large industrial communities. There has never been any harbour in the community, and it has never really had a pier for large vessels. In the nineteenth century, reference is found to a short pier at Skelmorlie, sailings from Greenock arriving at Skelmorlie Pier once per day in 1859, and in 1872 there was an auction of 'seven rowing and sailing boats, with oars, sails, moorings, and grapnels, hand and deep sea lines, nets, etc.' In 1869 two steamers, the *Sultan* and the *Vale of Clyde* collided off Wemyss Bay, the former being so damaged that she had to run for Skelmorlie Pier to land the passengers heading for Rothesay. The pier was located on the headland immediately west of where the hydropathic hotel once was, accessed via the lane in the middle of Shore Road terrace. In 1866 two beacons were erected near the pier to mark the start of a nautical mile, the second pair being position 6,080 feet to the south, near to Skelmorlie Castle. The beacons were 45 feet tall, and ships could check their speed by cruising past them and timing how long it took to line up the first pair until the lining up of the second pair. For a time there was a boat launch out into the bay from the roadside at Mira-Mar House, at the southern end of the community. This slip was around 270 yards in length. At the roadside a masonry slipway led down to the long slip. At the end of the slip was a perch. The slipway appears to have been constructed sometime between 1895 and 1909. A second jetty or boat launch was constructed at Chaseley House, further along the Largs road. It existed in 1895. Below Skelmorlie Castle, just north of Skelmorlie Bridge, a jetty extended out into the bay, existing at the turn of the twentieth century. On the landward end of the jetty was a boathouse, and adjacent to it was a tall flagstaff. Another boat house and slipway were located on the beach in front of Ashcraig House, at Meigle. Two boat slips existed on the shore below Knock Castle.

A Look Back at AYRSHIRE HARBOURS ~ page 9

Largs Harbour

The harbour at Largs has always been a small affair, with little more than a single pier and secondary breakwater. There was no pier here in the early nineteenth century, for nothing is shown on John Leslie's plan of Largs, dated 1811. At that time, boats used for transporting cattle or for fishing had either to draw up on the shingle beach, or attempt to land in the mouths of either the Gogo or Noddsdale waters. The foundation stone of the pier was laid on 10 January 1833 by William Miller. Construction took a year and the pier was first used on 1 December 1833. The cost was £4,275, the works undertaken by the Largs Harbour Company Ltd., which had 31 shareholders at £50 each. The pier extends about 300 feet west into the firth, with an almost right-angle bend extending 120 feet to the north. Just before the pier was opened to the public, a tragedy occurred which was to be one of the most distressing in the history of Clyde shipping. A ferry boat that was transferring passengers to the Hero was swamped with the backwash from the west wall of the pier. Seven or eight lives were lost. Parallel with the pier, to the north side of it, is what the 1855 Ordnance Survey map describes as a 'Low Water Landing Strip'. The two structures enclose a harbour of around 50,000 square feet. The first boat to land at the pier was the PS Glasgow, which had been built in 1813 by John Wood of Port Glasgow. In 1870 a new wooden corner was added to the pier. In 1882 and 1884 severe gales were to damage much of the pier. In the latter year the timber landing stage, which was added at the end of the stone pier, was wrecked. In the 1890s the harbour was purchased by the Glasgow and South Western Railway Company which had the intention of extending the railway line to the pier, which would have been rebuilt to cater for the increased number of passengers this was expected to create. However, there was much opposition to the proposals locally, and the railway plans were dropped. The use of the small pier became so intense during the hey-day of the Clyde steamers that a signal box was erected to control the ships that had to queue for a slot in which to land.

A Look Back at AYRSHIRE HARBOURS ~ page 11

Largs Ferry Port

Largs pier was purchased by the Caledonian Railway Company in November 1897. The pier was improved in 1903, when a new surface was laid on it. At the same time, it was extended very slightly. In 1923 the merging of the railway companies meant that Largs pier and harbour became the property of the London Midland and Scottish Railway. On Thursday 12 February 1931 there was an amazing sight when the largest ship ever to arrive at Largs pier was witnessed. The only thing is that it was not meant to be there! It had broken its moorings at Rothesay and was blown by a storm across the firth overnight. The three men on board were unable to steer it and had to await their fate. Chief officer Mr J. L. Nicol was quoted as saying, 'The manner in which the *Balgowan* drifted alongside Largs pier without human aid was a most remarkable happening. I thought nothing could prevent us from running aground on the Cumbrae or Ayrshire coast, and for a time, it was probable that we would strike the north end of Cumbrae, but when we got clear of the point it seemed we must ground on the Ayrshire coast.' Neither the ship, which had a gross tonnage of 6,599 tons, nor the pier suffered any real damage, and the vessel was able to be refloated at high tide with the aid of three tugs. Largs pier suffered damage in a storm in 1935, but the war years meant that it was not strengthened until 1948, at which time it was extended seawards for a further four and a half feet. In 1936 the pier was first used as the landward port of the Cumbrae ferry, when MV *Wee Cumbrae* started plying between Largs and the island. In 1970 a hovercraft operated from the pier to Cumbrae for a season, but it was not successful. The new ferry ramp was added in 1971-72, the new ferry service to Cumbrae which could take cars opening on 11 March 1972. The first vessels used were the MV *Coruisk* and MV *Kyleakin II*, which was to be renamed MV *Largs*. The most recent development was a £6m construction contract to build a new pier was awarded to George Leslie Ltd in September 2008; the project was completed in late 2009.

Largs ~ Cairnie's Quay

Cairnie's Quay is a concrete landing slip, located at Broomfield Crescent in Largs. It was probably constructed by Dr John Cairnie, who owned Curlinghall House on the esplanade behind it (erected in 1813). Certainly, during Cairnie's lifetime, the quay was used as a landing place for a 'cutter' that he owned, and which he used to bring granite from Ailsa Craig to Largs. This stone was then fashioned into curling stones, which were often used at the ice rink that he created at Curlinghall, hence the house's name. The quay is shown on a plan of Largs dated 1845. Largs Sailing Club was formed in 1936 by young men who failed to qualify for membership of the now defunct Royal Largs Yacht Club, which had a minimum age of 21 and be a master in his trade. The new yacht club was based in the old stable block of the Marine and Curlinghall Hotel (which had been established in Cairnie's old house), before moving to John Street in the early 1960s, and used the quay as their main base for sailing. In 1964 a Scottish Office Grant of £800 allowed several improvements to be made to the slip, and it is thought that it was widened around 1968. At one time the quay had a starter's hut at its landward side. The sailing club moved to Largs Yacht Haven (which was opened in 1984) in 1999, after which the slip was disused for a time. The quay is now operated and maintained by the Cairnie's Quay Mooring Association and is still used by small pleasure craft. Prior to Cairnie's Quay, this part of the coast at Largs had a small harbour with two breakwaters extending into the water. The harbour appears on old plans of the early nineteenth century. The harbour area was infilled around 1850 and the site of it is now occupied by the foreshore in front of Makerstoun Place. Various proposals for harbours in Largs were made over the centuries, including one in the proposed New Town of Largs in 1798, which was never developed. This would have had two arched breakwaters reaching into the firth from the promenade of the present Aubery Crescent with a central quay between them.

Fairlie Pier

In the mid-nineteenth century there were a few narrow piers at Fairlie, extending into the firth. One was located at Beach House, another off Ferry Row, and a third at Rockhaven, known as Knox's Quay. This last one was the original Cumbrae ferry terminal, the house behind known as the Ferry Inn before becoming Rockhaven. Early in the twentieth century they were joined by a few others. These 'landing piers' were used by both fishermen and boat-hirers, such as the MacMillan brothers, who also offered trips to the two Cumbrae islands. The pier at Fairlie was officially opened on 1 July 1882, shortly after the station, which opened on 10 June. A headland of rubble was pushed onto Fairlie Sands, at the end of which a T-shaped pier was built, 300 feet long by 40 feet in breadth, with a hammer head of 200 feet by 30 feet. A branch of the Ardrossan and Largs railway was extended into the pier, with Fairlie Pier Station opened at the same time. From here Messrs Hill & Co. operated steamers to Millport on Great Cumbrae and Kilchattan Bay on Bute. In August 1935 part of the timber pier went on fire, believed to have been started by a cigarette butt. The damage was estimated at £500. The pier was also used to land herring catches in the past, kippering sheds existing on the shore. During the Second World War ferries plied from the pier to Brodick on Arran. The railway station was closed on 31 July 1972, at the same time as steamer services from Fairlie Pier to Brodick and Tarbert were discontinued. The pier was subsequently demolished. To the north of the pier a second pier was constructed by NATO in the 1950s as a Boom Defence Base. This was used to prevent Russian submarines from making their way up the Firth of Clyde, towards sensitive sites such as Faslane. The base was also used to maintain buoys and moorings used by NATO ships mooring in the Clyde. Large sheds were erected, and a railway siding led to the pier. At the end of the 'Cold War,' the site was decommissioned and in 1995 purchased by Holt Leisure and converted into a marina and leisure boat facility.

Hunterston Terminal

The port of Hunterston is a relatively modern creation, dating from 1973-79, when British Steel acquired the Hunterston Sands and the adjoining shores. In 1970 a report entitled 'Oceanspan' was published by the Scottish Council for Development and Industry which envisaged the best deep-water port in Europe. Initial proposals included a £20 million steelworks and container terminal, however the steelworks never came to fruition, nor did an oil refinery for Chevron. A massive terminal was constructed with a pier pushed out into Fairlie Roads, which could allow ships of up to 350,000 tons to unload iron ore. Two massive cranes could empty the ships at a rate of 3,000 tons per hour. The cranes had a height of 236 feet. With a discharge rate of up to 50,000 tonnes of coal it was claimed to be the fastest in the United Kingdom. The port has a draught of over 115 feet and an outer quay length of around 500 yards. The iron ore was transferred to railway waggons which were moved to the steelworks of Ravenscraig in Lanarkshire. When Ravenscraig was closed in 1992, iron ore was no longer imported and the terminal was used solely for coal, which was then transported to various power stations. Initially, the plans envisaged a new steelworks on the flats to replace Ravenscraig and other steel production facilities around the east end of Glasgow and Motherwell, but campaigning by the workers prevented its construction and saved their own jobs, at least for some decades. A large dry dock was constructed, covering 88 acres, making it one of the largest in Europe. There were also plans to make Hunterston the largest deep-water container terminal in the north of Britain, but again these failed to come to fruition. The Hunterston terminal was taken over, along with the rest of Clydeport, by the Peel Group in 2003. The port was closed in 2016 at the same time as the closure of the Longannet Power Station and it lay dormant for several years. The large unloading cranes were removed in 2019. The huge site is currently being developed for commercial and industrial purposes. In 2022 plans were approved for a high voltage subsea cable manufacturing facility which would involve erecting a 600-feet tall extrusion tower.

Portencross Pier

On 23 December 1904 William Adams of Overton and Auchenames applied to the Board of Trade to become the harbour authority for Portencross Harbour and a proposed pier. The application stated that a new pier would be built, and the existing two harbours would be widened and dredged. The plan had been that the railway would have made its way along the coast by way of Portencross to Largs, and work on the pier started. The act would have allowed Adams to construct wharves, quays, and ancillary buildings, and to employ 'harbour masters, dock masters, pier masters, weighers, constables and other officers'. However, when the railway was rerouted elsewhere, the pier was abandoned half-built. It is said to have been only the second concrete pier constructed in the world. In 1906 proposals were made to construct a tramway from Portencross Pier along the coast, through West Kilbride, Ardrossan, Saltcoats and Stevenston to Nobel's chemical works at Ardeer, a distance of 11½ miles. This would allow passengers at the pier to travel to nearby towns, as well as workers from the towns to commute to Ardeer. It was never built. The pier was not completed until 1912, when workers on Auchenames estate finished it. It has a concrete block at the start, with a T-shaped jetty built of concrete extending into the open water. The pier was then used by several Clyde steamers over the years, including the Juno, which called in 1912. At the outbreak of war in 1914 the pier was abandoned by the pleasure boats and they did not return after the armistice. The pier was temporarily repaired in 1993 when the BBC used it for filming an adaptation of Neil Munro's novel, *Para Handy*. For this the pier was made to look as though it was still the 1930s. In 1994 the pier was sold by Scottish Nuclear, along with a strip of coastline southwards towards the old harbour, to Peter Kay, a businessman who owned part of Little Cumbrae. The company had previously considered demolishing the pier, regarding it as a liability. The last sea-going paddle steamer in the world, Waverley, called in 1995, following a major refit. The visit was to be the first by a pleasure steamer since 1913.

Portencross New Harbour

The new harbour at Portencross is in fact ancient in itself, but was not as old as the castle harbour. It was probably developed in the early nineteenth century as a fishing station. It has a couple of stone-built walls and mooring posts. The seaward side of the harbour has a pier, accessed from the south, built with the benefit of surrounding rocks. The harbour dries out when the tide is out, leaving the small vessels that still use it perched on sand or gravel. The New Harbour was developed for fishing boats, though only small vessels were ever able to make use of its limited sheltered anchorage. At the start of the eighteenth century it is thought that the thirty fishing boats in West Kilbride parish were based at Portencross old harbour. In the late eighteenth century this harbour was in serious decline as it could only take vessels up to 50 tons burden. By 1820 the fishing had declined at Portencross, and there were only seven wherries based there, employing nineteen. Some fishing continued, however, and salmon fishing, using nets placed in the bay, took place up until the 1960s. There have been several interesting events associated with the harbour. One of these took place on Thursday 15 December 1859 a boat left the harbour at around half past three in the afternoon. On board were Henry MacConnell, a labourer, and Samuel Lewis, a stonemason, complete with the load of lime and stone. They were employed by George Robertson, builder, West Kilbride. The men were headed for Little Cumbrae, where they were to complete some building works. The boat was known to be leaky, but it was observed sailing satisfactorily past the half-way point between the harbour and the island. After that the vessel disappeared, and no trace of the boat nor the men was found again. It is reckoned that owing to the condition of the boat and its heavy cargo, that they sank to the bottom of the sea. The New, or North Harbour, is owned by the Portencross Harbour Trust. Several locals were concerned about the possibility of a developer purchasing the harbour and immediate surroundings and blocking open access, so decided to form a trust to acquire the basin.

Portencross Old Harbour

The old harbour at Portencross was associated with the castle, being located immediately north of the ancient tower. It may be late mediaeval in date. It dries out at low tide. An old custom has it that the harbour of Portencross was the chosen spot for funeral corteges carrying the dead Scottish monarchs on their way to burial on the island of Iona. Tradition claims that they came from Edinburgh by way of Paisley and Kilmacolm, before arriving at West Kilbride, where the street Halfway, or 'Haaf Way' recalls the route followed. At Portencross the monarch or his close family's coffins were transferred from being carried on a horse-drawn carriage to a sailing ship that would take the corpse around Kintyre and out to the sacred isle. Monarchs traditionally passing through Portencross include Kenneth MacAlpine and Malcolm Canmore. A later maritime association that Portencross has is with the Spanish Armada of Philip II of 1588. This sailed around Scotland from the eastern side, heading down the west coast, trying to make a way home following defeat by the English. Many of the ships were sunk in the stormy weather, and it is believed that one of them sunk in ten fathoms of water off the coast of Portencross. There are claims that the local Gemmell family are descended from survivors who made it to the shore. The enigma of the ship has played on idle minds ever since, and there have been various attempts at finding it, and perhaps the treasure it is supposed to have contained. One of the attempts at finding the vessel took place in August 1740 by an expedition by Sir Archibald Grant of Monymusk and Captain Roe. A diving bell was used to reach the wreck. What was brought up from the sea bed were some old cannons, one of which was for many years positioned by the harbour side. On it the Spanish arms were discernible in the early nineteenth century. With the iron gun eroding in the salt-water spray, the cannon was moved in 1989 to the museum area of Hunterston Power Station. It was later located outside the power station offices. Other cannons lifted from the sea bed were sent to Edinburgh Castle and the Tower of London.

Ardrossan Harbour

Unlike most harbours in Ayrshire, the foundation date of Ardrossan's is known. The port was established by Hugh Montgomerie, 12th Earl of Eglinton, on 31 July 1806. His intention was that it would become the new port for Glasgow, for the Clyde was at that time shallow and difficult to navigate. To transport goods from the port to the city the Glasgow, Paisley and Johnstone Canal was proposed, but this was never completed. The oldest part of the harbour was the dock and tidal basin. The former was protected by a new pier on its western side, and wharves allowed vessels to berth. A lock of two gates allowed vessels to reach the wet dock. Lord Eglinton's works were halted in 1815 when costs passed £100,000. Thomas Telford and John Rennie were looking for a further £300,000 to complete the works. In 1833 work on the harbour restarted, when the 13th Earl came of age. A further £200,000 was spent on the port, cut back from the original proposals. In 1833 the Arran mail boat commenced, also offering passenger and cargo services. The harbour prospered, 2,000 vessels using it each year. In 1836 60,000 tons of coal was exported. The Wet Dock was built in 1845. In 1886 the harbour was taken over by the Ardrossan Harbour Company, with Lord Eglinton the major shareholder. A new dock was constructed, named the Eglinton Dock, which extends to 10 acres and a depth of 27 feet. Adjoining this is the Eglinton Tidal basin. These were opened on 4 April 1892. New railway stations were built on the piers, the Montgomerie Pier Station to the north, the Winton Pier Station to the south, both named after Lord Eglinton's family. At the same time a new breakwater 1,320 feet long, was constructed across the mouth of the harbour, protecting it from the west. Incorporated in this was the Crinan Rock. The harbour was very busy, with 2,923 vessels using it in 1894. The ships exported and imported goods from France, United States, Portugal and Spain. Principal exports were coal and pig iron. Imports included timber, grain, limestone, iron ore and pyrites. Fishing boats also used the harbour, in 1890 108 boats were based here, rising to 200 in the 1920s.

Ardrossan Shipyard

The old dock had a shipbuilding yard on its southern side, with a slipway and graving dock, the latter capable of taking ships of 1,500 tons. Early shipbuilders in the town included Barclay and Archibald Boyd. Barr & Shearer operated the shipyard until 1885, when it was taken over by Ardrossan Shipbuilding Company. In 1926 this company was reconstituted as Ardrossan Dockyard Ltd. The shipyard had eight building berths and modern facilities for constructing ships, or for carrying out repairs. In 1931 the Ardrossan Dockyard Ltd was acquired by National Shipbuilders Security Ltd. The South Shipyard was dismantled and the property sold off. Shipbuilding continued at Ardrossan until 1987, when the last vessel was launched. In 1927 Shell Oil built an oil storage depot and refinery on the north side of the harbour, and large tankers berthed at Montgomerie Pier. On reclaimed land many circular oil storage tanks were erected and railway sidings allowed tanker carriages to be filled. Imports of crude oil reached its peak in 1968, when 950,000 tons were pumped ashore. The refinery was to close in 1986 and the site was gradually redeveloped. The Earl of Eglinton sold his remaining shares in the harbour company to Colville's, the steel-making company, in 1930, bringing an end to the Eglinton connection with the port. In the 1920s 27 herring boats operated from the harbour. Fishing boats left the harbour in 1939, when the Admiralty commandeered the port to establish HMS Pactolus, a submarine depot. At the return of peace, the former fishermen were offered either compensation for their boats, or else their return. Most opted for the cash, and thus the fishing trade at Ardrossan died. The old dock and part of the old tidal basin were filled in when they were no longer commercially viable, leaving just the Eglinton dock and basin. The former was closed in 1995 and in 1997 converted into the Clyde Marina, the shipping which formerly used it having gone elsewhere. Ardrossan was also used for steamers, vessels leaving for Liverpool, Londonderry, Dublin and Belfast. The Arran ferry still uses the rebuilt Winton Pier. Ardrossan Harbour Company was sold to Clyde Port Authority in 1970, and is now owned by Peel Ports. An extension to the marina was proposed in 2022.

King Orry leaving Ardrossan

Ardrossan was used as a terminus for the ferry from Scotland to Douglas on the Isle of Man. This was established to promote holidays, and as such the service only took place in the summer months. The first vessel to sail the route was the *Peveril*, commencing in 1892. The photograph shows the SS *King Orry* leaving dock. This vessel was constructed in 1946 by Cammell Laird & Co, measuring 344 feet long with a tonnage of 2,485. Operated by the Isle of Man Steam Packet Company, the vessel remained in use until 1972, when it was replaced by *Mona's Queen*, and it was put out of service in 1975. The ferry service to Douglas ceased on 25 August 1985 due to a drop in demand. However, from 1994-1996 the *Claymore* was operated in the summer months by Caledonian MacBrayne from Ardrossan to the Isle of Man, taking eight hours, but due to new international passenger certificate regulations introduced after the sinking of the *Estonia* in the Baltic Sea, the service was withdrawn. It was CalMac's first service to extend outwith Scottish waters. The vessel is captured heading out the Eglinton Tidal Basin, with the Montgomerie Pier Station building to the right. This station was opened on 30 May 1890 by the Lanarkshire and Ayrshire Railway, later to become the Caledonian Railway Company. The station remained in use until 18 April 1966. Between the station buildings and the ferry can be made out one of the round oil tanks belonging to the Shell oil refinery. This was constructed from 1925-1927, and major dredging took place on the north side of Montgomerie Pier to allow large tankers to berth and unload. The vessel partially seen to the left was the *Lion*. This served the Northern Ireland passage from 3 January 1968 until 12 February 1976. The vessel was a 3,333-ton vessel, 364 feet long, able to carry up to 1,200 passengers and 176 cars. It later served the route from Dover to Boulogne, a spell in Greece, the Channel Islands, Israel and Indonesia, before being broken up in 2004. The first regular service to Northern Ireland commenced in 1884 when the Ardrossan Steam Navigation Company plied the *Glowworm* to Belfast.

Saltcoats Harbour from the Pier

The harbour at Saltcoats may have been established around 1683 when salt pans were created in the vicinity, and coal was exported from local mines. Robert Cuninghame was given the right to collect excise on all retailed brandy and whisky in Ardrossan and Stevenston parishes – he used much of the funds to develop Saltcoats harbour. The *Statistical Account* of 1791 includes a plan of proposed works to the harbour. It was noted that the basin was divided between two proprietors – Robert Reid Cuninghame in Stevenston parish and the Earl of Eglinton in Ardrossan parish. Eglinton's property was not developed, and it was noted that if that half was 'bassoned out, would make a spacious harbour and the same depth of water as in the Old South Harbour.' Plans also included a new street, and a carpenter yard (or shipbuilding yard) with a harbour frontage of 300 feet. The Old South Harbour was in use, with a harbour wall 500 feet long, protecting the basin. Plans were drawn up for an extension to the pier, around 220 feet in length, with a return pier 170 feet long. This would enclose a new outer basin, which would have had deeper water. Only part of the proposals on the Stevenston half of the harbour were carried out, the return pier not built. By 1800 it was reckoned that there were 41 vessels registered to the port. Around 1856 a railway was laid to the Old Pierhead, two tracks running along the back of the pier to the end. At various points turntables allowed waggons to be rotated and led to the edge of the quay, to allow tipping into boats. The railway was used to transport materials to the Ardeer Chemical Company. The rails were lifted sometime before 1895. At the pierhead was a 'lighthouse' which comprised of an iron structure which contained an iron cage, in which were placed live coals. When the winds blew stronger, the air fanned the coals, causing them to burn even more brighter. In 1882 the harbour was in a poor condition, and locals complained that A. W. R. Cuninghame of Auchenharvie did not maintain it, despite earning £150 per annum from it. Saltcoats Town Council made regular proposals to buy the harbour from the lairds.

Saltcoats Harbour Custom House

Saltcoats harbour comprises two basins, the Inner and Outer harbours, separated by the Old Pierhead. The pier extends from the end of Quay Street in a south-westerly direction for 280 yards, built on a stretch of rock known as The Shott and the Shottend. The Old Pierhead is the name of a transverse arm of around 50 yards, originally the extremity of the harbour. At a later date, the New Pier was extended further to the south-west, just short of the tidal rock known as the Inner Nebbock. There are no other piers or breakwaters. The pier was built around 1800. At the end of the pier an ornamental tower was erected in 1912. Saltcoats Harbour's inner basin is dry sand and shingly at low tide, only the more exposed outer harbour remaining under water. The harbour was rebuilt in 1914. Saltcoats harbour suffered considerably with the development of nearby Ardrossan harbour. Latterly, only small craft used it, but in recent years no boats are berthed there at all. Built on the pier was a Quay House, a double-storey building backing onto the breakwater, the front facing the harbour. The building was to become a public house, occupied by Jean Campbell up to 1860. Whilst it was a public house it had a kitchen, three rooms and four stores. It was demolished in 1924. Further along was the Harbour Office, or custom house, which was for a time a maritime museum. In 1939 the Ordnance Survey map indicates a monument near where the Quay House stood. Building boats was carried on at Saltcoats. There were at least three yards in the eighteenth century, located on the Braes, where ships were built on timber slips. When complete, the vessels were hauled down to the harbour at high tide. Shipbuilders in Saltcoats included William Ritchie, who was active from around 1775 to 1790. He later moved to Belfast where he opened a larger shipyard. Mr Murphy had a large yard in the early nineteenth century, building Dublin brigs from oak for the coal trade. He later moved to a bigger yard at Greenock. A dock on the braes was used for building fishing smacks and wherries, reached by a channel cut through the rocks. By 1815 shipbuilding at Saltcoats had expired.

Saltcoats Harbour looking seaward

The quay at Saltcoats could afford a depth of 13 feet of water at high water spring tides. In January 1739 a storm destroyed much of the pier but it was rebuilt within two weeks by ten masons who were paid tenpence and a tot of whisky per day. By 1843 the harbour was governed by trustees, an Act of Parliament of that year confirming this. In 1847 the harbour hosted 215 vessels, totalling 15,873 tons, the revenue being £166. There were eighteen fishing vessels based there. At one time the harbour had a lighthouse keeper and pilot, this position being carried out by James MacDonald, a hero of Camperdown who was held prisoner for eighteen months by the French. He served in the merchant navy until his retiral in 1851, from when he served as lighthouse keeper until his death in 1869, aged 96. Complaints on the upkeep of the harbour were often made to the local press, such as in 1882 when it was noted that 'through wilful neglect it has, for a long period past, been slowly going to the bad, and the terrible storms of this winter have completed its ruin'. In 1914 the harbour was acquired by Saltcoats Town Council from Captain Cuninghame and work on repairing it commenced, which included building the new tower at the pier end. A bronze plaque bears the inscription, *Saltcoats Harbour, erected under Act of Scots Parliament, 1686; enlarged 1797; purchased by the Town and renovated, 1914*. The council paid £2,000 for the harbour and by September 1915 spent a further £3,808 on restoration work. Along the Braes were shipyards, building smallish boats. Between 1775 and 1790 sixty-four ships were built. In 1877 the shipyard at Saltcoats was offered for sale. In October 1891 a great storm created a breach twelve feet wide in the harbour wall, washing away part of the roadway. In 1962 an amateur geologist and teacher at Glengarnock, Matthew Yuille, discovered 26 fossilized tree trunks in the shingle on the west side of the harbour. Evidence of these can still be found when the tide is out. In 2019 a Saltcoats Harbour Association was formed by locals keen to bring the harbour back into use but the charity folded in 2023.

Ardeer Wharf

Although there is no harbour at Ardeer, there were various proposals to construct one over the years. One of these dates from 1883. Messrs. Merry & Cuninghame, the local coal and ironmasters, proposed building a breakwater and harbour which would be convenient for their furnaces. The plans were renewed in 1885, and an application sent to Irvine Harbour Trustees indicating a desire to take over the foreshore and adjoining ground. The company had proposed depositing blast furnace slag to create the breakwater, and a harbour subsequently created within it. In 1894 another scheme to build a pier was proposed by Nobel's Explosives Company Ltd. This was for a pier about 650 yards long, 'consisting of cast-iron piles, steel work, timber and concrete.' The pier was designed by Messrs Crouch & Hogg of Glasgow. Plans for a pier were made in 1905 and work on it commenced – the foundation stone being laid at midday on 1 January 1907. This was a low-key affair – the foundation stone being a block of slag from the ironworks. Initial plans indicate two piers projecting into the water, the westmost curving towards the east to form a harbour. The proposals were scaled back, and only a dumped pile of slag was ever created, although by the 1960s a slip allowed boats to launch. Irvine Harbour Trust objected to the plans, reckoning that the new port would compete for trade. The pier was completed to its maximum extent by 1910 and soon became a popular spot for bathers. On Sunday 19 June 1910 a miner, Isaac Maxwell, aged 18, jumped from the pier into ten feet of water. He was unable to swim and his friend was unsuccessful in trying to rescue him. On the opposite side of the peninsula the Nobel Harbour, or Garnock Wharf, was established in 1905, located on the River Garnock. Earlier attempts to establish a harbour here in 1875 and 1881 came to nought – Irvine Harbour Trust demanding a charge of two shillings and sixpence per ton of material offloaded. The later wharf was opened in 1908. A railway linked the pier with the remainder of the works. When explosives were being moved at the wharf, attendance at the Magnum Leisure Centre was restricted, for safety reasons. Ships used the wharf until the 1990s.

Irvine Harbour

It is claimed that the Romans had a port at Irvine, used to supply their soldiers from ships that plied up the west coast of Britain. However, no evidence of this survives, and the mouths of the rivers Irvine and Garnock have moved around over the centuries, the sandy dunes blocking the confluences at different periods. The original harbour, at least known to history, was located near the town itself, probably around the Low Green area, at Seagatefoot, for the opposite side of the river was in the parish of Dundonald, and thus beyond the control of the burgh. Irvine harbour always suffered from sand – in 1565 a report said that it was 'not verye good', and in 1604-8 Timothy Pont noted that the harbour was 'now much decayed from quhat it was anciently, being stopt with shelves of sand which hinders the neir approach of shipping'. In the seventeenth century the town's sailors complained of the silting of the harbour, preventing vessels from sailing readily to the wharves. In 1572 new wharves were constructed at Marress, and the port was able to import goods from Bordeaux, the Netherlands and Scandinavia. In 1665 plans were made for creating a new channel for the boats, but the idea was probably abandoned when, in 1677, the burgh got the right to the channel of the Irvine opposite the foot of the Garnock, and a new quay was constructed. Silting remained a problem, and the river was dredged in 1735. A new quay was erected in 1739 and in 1755 it was decided to sink wooden palings into the river to constrain it, thus creating a faster flow which was hoped would help clear the channel of sand. In 1751 the town bought its first dredger, under the command of the 'shoremaster' or harbour master, an appointment first made in 1731. The harbour was busy with vessels exporting coal, 24,000 tons by 1791, as well as goods produced in Glasgow, Paisley and Kilmarnock. The importation of tobacco was popular for a while, before the ships became too large for the harbour to cope with. The quay was extended in 1790 but the lack of water at the bar meant that larger ships were soon to abandon the harbour in favour of the more accessible port at Ardrossan.

Irvine Dredger Operators

The first known ship-building yard in Irvine was established in 1759, when John Webb took on a feu and started building timber vessels. He was later joined by John Martin's yard and Gilkison, Thomson & Co. A single slip dropped into the river from the yard. David Gilkison had a son, William (1777-1833), who founded the Canadian town Elora. In 1886 D. McGill took over and remained owner until 1892 when J. H. Gilmour had it for a couple of years. In 1898 the Irvine Shipbuilding and Engineering Company was formed, and it operated the shipbuilding yard until 1904. The council took over the yard and in 1912 leased it to Mackie and Thomson of Govan. Four large berths were constructed and a patent slipway installed by Messrs. MacBride & Co. of Port Glasgow in 1913. Ships up to 10,000 tons could be built, and over 700 men were gainfully employed. The shipyard and much of the harbour was taken over by Ayrshire Dockyard Company in 1919. The *Clan MacTaggart* and *Clan MacTavish* were built for the Clan Line, at 7,610 tons each they were the largest ever constructed at Irvine. In 1928 the yard was taken over by Sir J. & H. Lithgow. The last ships, the *Coulmore* and *Culbeg*, were built in 1936, but the yard continued to carry out repairs during and immediately after the war. The yard was taken over by Ayrshire Metals Ltd in 1961 and became an engineering company before closing totally. In 1847 the first railway siding was laid down to the harbour, and to accommodate unloading onto ships a new Coal Shipping Wharf was built. A second line allowed carriages to be taken to a point at the Upper Wharf. In 1873 the harbour trustees developed the harbour considerably, introducing new steam cranes, which increased the coal trade. The Upper Wharf was extended westwards to join the Coal Wharf, creating a lengthy stretch of mooring, serviced by a railway siding and later by a travelling crane. In 1935 the harbour was purchased by ICI, which had a massive chemical and explosives plant at Ardeer, on the opposite side of the river. The harbour was later sold to NPL Estates and is no longer used as a commercial port.

The *Garnock* in Irvine Harbour

Facing the harbour runs Harbour Street, the south side of which is lined with buildings old and new. Among the old are the Ship Inn, established in 1750 by Charles Hamilton, one of the burgh's provosts, and the Harbour Master's Office. In recent years a sculpture of a carter with his horse has been erected here, the work of David Annand. The depth of water at the harbour bar was always a problem for Irvine mariners. In 1906 the harbour master, Martin Boyd (1846-1918), invented an automatic depth signalling device which was constructed at the mouth of the river. Known as the Pilot House, the tower had pulleys and ropes within it, controlled by rising and falling floats in the water. Balls on a mast indicated the depth of water at the Bar, and at night-time blinds obliterated lights in windows, indicating the same information. The building was officially opened on 23 May 1906. Once it was declared open, the party sailed to Largs and returned in the evening, entering the harbour at night to see the pilot house signals in operation. Near the south pier was a lifeboat house, erected in 1874, though the first lifeboat was gifted in 1833. The *Busbie* was a noted lifeboat used in the rescue of the crew of the Norwegian ship, the *Frey*. The coxswain, David Sinclair, and the crew were later rewarded by the King of Norway. In 1983 the Scottish Maritime Museum was established at Irvine, with a ship-building shed relocated from Linthouse, Govan, in 1991. Wharves allow various heritage vessels to be visited, and there is a visitor centre and café at the head of the harbour. Vessels maintained by the museum include the *Spartan*, a Clyde puffer, and the *Garnock*, the harbour tug. 'The Big Idea' was established on the Ardeer peninsula, with the Bridge of Scottish Inventions across the harbour lining it to Irvine. The bridge could retract to allow vessels to pass through. The first sod of the science centre was cut by Dr Michael Nobel on 21 September 1998 and it was opened on 15 April 2000. The attraction closed in 2003 due to a lack of visitors and a future for the building has still to be found.

Troon Harbour

There was a small fishing station at Troon for many years before the present harbour was developed. In 1608 the Burgh of Irvine proposed constructing a new harbour at the 'Trone' to replace its own silted haven. After a few years the Irvine port was repaired and the Troon scheme abandoned. In 1707 Colonel William Fullarton obtained a charter from Queen Anne allowing him to develop a harbour 'with power to uplift anchorage and other customs' and a canal to Kilmarnock, but this came to nought. As late as 1804, an old plan of Fullarton Estate indicates a small 'Harbour' on the east side of Troon point, and the village of Troon comprised of little more than a row of cottages, no doubt occupied by fishermen. A slightly later estate map of 1806 does not show a harbour, indicating that there was probably little more than a landing point on the shore. The present harbour at Troon was developed from 1808 by the 4th Duke of Portland, William Jessop being the principal engineer. A quay 500 feet long was built into the bay, perpendicular to the headland. In 1817 the North Pier was extended in a north-easterly direction, into 19 feet of water. An eastern wall was built to stop the sand-drift from Irvine Bay. A new quay was added in 1832. The harbour light was erected in 1837. In 1840 a new West Dock was cut out from the solid rock. A long East Pier was reconstructed from Temple Hill, heading parallel with the Troon point, sheltering the outer and inner harbours. Initially, this was just an artificial island, nicknamed 'St Helena' after the island where Napoleon was imprisoned, but it was gradually linked to the shore and extended towards the harbour mouth. At the west end of the outer harbour a West Pier was built in a northerly direction, protecting the large basins from westerly winds. Alongside the Outer Harbour a wet dock was excavated, extending to just over two acres. This had an entrance 49 feet wide and was completed in 1846. In 1846 the harbour saw 2,436 vessels arrive, a total of 184,826 tons. In 1863 Troon was designated the head port of the port of Irvine.

Troon Fishing Boats

In 1901 Troon harbour was sold by the Duke of Portland to the Glasgow and South Western Railway Company. This firm introduced several pleasure steamers to the port, particularly the *Juno*, which was in service from 1898 until 1932. She was replaced by the *Duchess of Hamilton* (until 1939) and then by the *Marchioness of Graham* (until 1947). These steamers took tourists across the Firth of Clyde and to various Clyde and Argyll ports. The railway company successors remained as owners of the harbour until 1 January 1950 when it was acquired by the Docks & Inland Waterways Executive. In 1963 it was transferred to the British Transport Docks Board. In 1983 the harbour became the property of Associated British Ports. It continues to import timber from Argyll and is the home port for several fishing boats, amongst these being those operated by Coastal Shellfish, which supplies clams, lobster and crabs to restaurants across the country. The first lifeboat station at Troon was erected in 1870 on ground in Portland Street, granted by the Duke of Portland. The first lifeboat cost £500. This was the *Mary Sinclair*, which served the port from 1871-1886. It was followed by the *Alexander Munnoch* (1886-1899), *Charles Skirrow* (1899-1904), *Busbie* (1904-1929), *Sir David Richmond* (1929-1955), *James & Barbara Aitken* (1955-1968), *Connell Elizabeth Cargill* (1968-1985), *Augustine Courtauld* (1985-1987), *City of Glasgow III* (1987-2004), and *Jim Moffat* (2004-present). Troon Marina was established in the Inner Harbour in 1978 and became Troon Yacht Haven in 1994. It now has berths for 400 boats. On the seaward side of the North Pier a terminal for the P&O ferry to Larne in Northern Ireland was constructed, allowing vehicles to be driven on board the catamaran. The service lasted from 2003 until 2016. At times the terminal has been used for the Arran ferry, during inclement weather and whilst Ardrossan was being upgraded. Troon Cruising Club was formed in 1955 by a number of small boat owners. They took over the former Seaman's Mission as their clubhouse and in 1976 built a pontoon in the Inner Harbour. A new clubhouse was erected in 1980. The Troon Sailing Club was formed in 1958, but folded in 1992. Troon Coastal Rowing Club was formed in 2011.

Troon Shipyard

On the south side of the Outer Harbour a shipyard was established in 1810-11 by the Duke of Portland and many timber-hulled vessels were launched from the yard. These included the Clown, built for the Duke himself, as well as the 50-ton smack Fullarton which was launched on 2 September 1818. In 1822 the Duke of Portland had his own 101 cutter built at the yard. Pantaloon, a 323-ton vessel with ten guns, was launched on 20 June 1831. The vessel was placed on trial with the Admiralty, and she was subsequently purchased by them and used to pursue pirates off the North African coast. To either side of the yard graving docks were excavated, in existence by 1828. One of these was 37 feet wide, the other 24 feet wide. There were three building slips, In 1843 the Duke of Portland sold the yard to the Troon Shipbuilding Company and by 1847 the yard employed 100 men. This firm built numerous timber vessels such as schooners around 200 tons in size on spec. In 1887 the yard was acquired by the Ailsa Shipbuilding Company when it moved from its smaller yard at Maidens. The first vessel constructed by it was the *Herald of Mercy*, a small 10-ton wooden ketch. Around 1900 the east graving dock was rebuilt at an angle to the Inner Harbour, allowing larger ships to be berthed. In 1902 the *Scotia* was built for the National Antarctic Expedition. The Ailsa shipyard built almost 600 vessels, including minesweepers, frigates, and several ferries for Caledonian MacBrayne, such as the *Iona* and *Lochmor*. The yard was nationalised in 1977 and became part of British Shipbuilders Corporation. In 1981 it became part of Ferguson-Ailsa, linked with the yard at Port Glasgow. The shipyard was privatised once more in 1986 as Ailsa & Perth, and the first fishing vessel built by it, the *Aeolus*, was launched in 1997. The last vessel, the ferry *Lochnevis*, was launched on 8 May 2000. The shipyard was closed that year and its site was taken over by Alexanders Timber Designs, manufacturer of timber frame houses and trusses. In addition, the West of Scotland Shipbuilding Co. Ltd. existed at the harbour, much of its work being in the breaking up of redundant vessels. Pictured is HMS *Aberdare*, launched at Troon on 29 April 1918.

Ayr Harbour

The harbour in the mouth of the River Ayr has been in existence since time immemorial. Shipbuilding is first mentioned in 1236, when Alexander II granted a charter allowing the use of timber from the lands of Alloway and others for the use of housebuilding and boat-building. In 1315 Edward Bruce is recorded as having sailed from Ayr to Ireland. Export and import of goods took place from early times, and in the fifteenth century reference is made to wine being brought from France. In 1528 is the first reference to the export of coal from the harbour, something that was to continue for centuries thereafter. There is reference to a fish market in Ayr as early as 1538. Major works on the harbour took place from 1587 after a period of severe neglect. In 1599 a new quay was built, but by 1604 a stent was levied on the inhabitants of the burgh for repairs. At the beginning of the seventeenth century, Ayr was regarded as being the third most important port in Scotland. The Ratton Quays on the south side of the river were rebuilt in 1713. In 1771 James Watt was consulted on harbour improvements, and he suggested extending the two piers seaward on either side of the river mouth. In 1772 John Smeaton suggested that the north pier should be slightly curved. John Rennie advised in 1805 – suggesting the piers be extended and that the former Newton Loch be converted into a wet dock. The only proposals from this list to come into fruition was the partial extension of the north pier in 1800 and the extension and rebuilding of the south pier in 1825. In 1830 Robert Stevenson surveyed the harbour and suggested extending the North Pier, plus other improvements within the harbour. In 1836 a rubble-stone breakwater, 133 yards long, was constructed beyond the north pier head, designed by John Gibb, engineer. The lighthouse was erected in 1841, designed by Robert Paton, and adjoining it was a short pier projecting into the bay, later to be incorporated into the wharf next to the dock. In 1846 the harbour had a total wharfage of 1,200 yards, and a crane capable of lifting six tons. In 1845 60 yards of the north quay were rebuilt.

Ayr Fishing Boats

The north side of the River Ayr was outwith the Royal Burgh's control, and thus was initially developed by the residents of Newton-upon-Ayr, much to the disgust of the royal burghers. In 1835 the Harbour Trust was formed, with representatives from Ayr and Newton councils, as well as shipowners and merchants. After Newton was subsumed into the control of Ayr council, the harbour was developed as one, and in 1866-78 a new wet dock of over six acres in extent was excavated on the Newton side. Previously this had been the site of a shipbuilding yard, patent slip, dry dock, and termini of railway sidings, abutting onto the wharf. The dock cost £165,000, the cost underwritten by James Baird of Cambusdoon. The stone for the walls was quarried from within the dock itself, all designed by Thomas Meek, engineer. The Slip Dock on the south side was built in 1883. A second proposed dock was planned for the area of York Street, east of the ship-building yard, but it was never excavated. The wharves commenced at the end of Darlington Place, and lined North Harbour Street as far as the Pilot House. Near to the shipyard a railway siding allowed wagons to be brought alongside moored ships, and beyond the yard four railheads allowed wagons to be emptied directly into the holds. The shipyard on the north side of the harbour was latterly operated by Sloan and Gemmel. It had a dry dock and patent slip. The yard was noted for its wooden-hulled vessels, in particular sailing clippers. One of the more celebrated vessels launched there was the Felix (1850), built for the Arctic explorer, Sir John Ross. The yard closed in the 1880s and became a timber mill for Messrs. Paton. In the late nineteenth century the harbour was bustling, with imports of slate, beef, limestone, timber and porter matched by exports of coal (500,000 tons in 1900, 1.1 million tonnes in 1991), pig iron, leather and ale. The harbour was transferred to the Glasgow and South Western Railway Company on 28 March 1919 and became the property of British Railways in 1948. In 1950 it became part of the Docks and Inland Waterways executive and from 1983 was part of Associated British Ports.

Ayr Ships and Fishing

A lifeboat station was established in 1803 and a lifeboat with ten oars was acquired with a grant of £50 from Lloyd's Society. A lifeboat house was erected at the end of South Harbour Street, near the junction with South Beach Road, and noted lifeboats in the town included three named *Janet Hoyle*. The station was closed in 1932 and the area served by the station at Troon. The *Janet Hoyle* of 1910 was rescued by the Thames Ironworks Heritage Trust in 2013, with plans to restore it. The shipyard on the south side of the harbour was built in 1883 by the Glasgow firm of MacKnight, MacCredie & Company. When MacCredie retired in the 1880s the yard was run by Samuel MacKnight, who lived nearby in Seabank Road, overlooking the yard. The first iron vessel built in Ayr was launched there in September 1883, the *Elach Hall*. Other ships built by that firm included the *Madge Wildfire* (1886) and *Chieftain* (1907). The largest vessel launched in Ayr was the *Straits of Gibraltar*, an iron screw steamer 281 feet long, 37 feet in breadth, and 23 feet 6 inches in depth with a displacement of 2,000 tons. In 1902 Samuel MacKnight & Co. was bought over by Ailsa Shipbuilding Company. The last ship to be built at Ayr was the *Ville de Papeete*, which was launched on 14 November 1928. The depression followed, and shipbuilding never returned. From 1941 until 1947 the yard was operated by the London Graving Dock Co. on behalf of the Admiralty Merchant Shipbuilding and Repair Department for repairing navy vessels. Hundreds of ships passed through the yard during this period. In 1947 the yard was taken over by the Ayr Engineering and Constructional Co. The fishmarket in Ayr was closed in 1996 and the fishing fleet relocated to Troon. To commemorate the history of the fishing industry in Ayr a statue of a fisherman holding a fish was erected at the Fish Cross, the traditional site of the market in Ayr for sea produce. The port of Ayr continues to be busy, with over 340,000 tonnes of cargo passing through, including grain, salt, turbines and timber. It is also used for cruise liner embarkations.

Dunure Harbour

The small harbour at Dunure is today an attractive basin, measuring 230 feet by 160 feet, surrounded by stone walls. The natural gap in the rocks was probably used for many years (a creek where boats landed was noted in 1655) before 1810-11 when Thomas Kennedy of Dunure commissioned Charles Abercrombie to construct the present harbour. This involved blasting some rock away and using the stone to build piers, and excavating a fifty-yard-wide channel leading to it. It is estimated that the cost was around £50,000. *An act for erecting and maintaining a harbour and works connected therewith at Dunure in the county of Ayr, 6th May 1811,* allowed work to continue. The western pier is the most significant, protecting the rectangular basin from the sea. At its northern extremity is a tapered round pillar, now severely worn by the salt air. It does not appear to have ever had a light on it, though some say that it did contain a burning beacon on occasions. The north pier is less-refined than the other piers – it replaced an older pier located further north. Early plans for the harbour included the construction of warehouses on the west and east sides of the basin, with the north pier being a wide space on which were to be established timber yards, building slips, and a dry dock. Sites around the harbour were identified as being suitable for building houses, but only really that on the south side was developed initially. The basin was blasted from the rock to a level base which was covered over with puddle clay to form a cushion layer. The first vessel engaging in trade to use the new harbour was the sloop *Carrick*, captained by MacNidar, which arrived in August 1811 with a cargo of slates from the island of Easdale in Argyll. At the time the boat entered the harbour there was thirteen feet of water on the bar. The harbour was actually proposed to be used for the export of coal from the Ayrshire mines, but its location was rather too far from the main coalfields and the trade did not take off. Instead, the harbour became used by fishermen but by 1886 Francis Groome noted that it had fallen into decay.

Approaching Dunure Harbour

In 1897 the harbour was improved to plans by the engineer H. V. Eaglesham. This involved widening the entrance and deepening the basin. Dunure harbour was at one time used for exporting coal. This was mined at a pit near to Fisherton School, but the enterprise was never as successful as other Ayrshire mines. Instead, in 1819, leases were offered for plots where 'a most advantageous fishing station and a place where various trades may be carried on, and a considerable intercourse by shipping may be established.' The harbour was then mainly used by fishermen, and many boats would use it for landing haddock and whiting. The Dunure Harbour Commission continued to make improvements to the basin, and in October 1923 advertised for contractors who could remove about 460 cubic yards of rock from the entrance channel to the harbour. Fishing vessels that used the harbour in the 1930s included the *Nancy* and the *Ermine*. Deaths and drownings continued to take place amongst the fishermen of Dunure. On 28 February 1906 a fishing boat was making an entry to the harbour when it was struck by a large wave which overturned it. One of those on board, Hugh Thomson, aged 75, was drowned. As fishing boats increased their draught, the basin became too shallow for it to be used, When the main fishing fleet moved to deeper water at either Ayr or Girvan, Dunure was left to pleasure craft, plus a few lobster boats. The inshore fishing industry continued to exist at Dunure harbour for a number of years after the war, but it fell into decline and by the 1960s had almost stopped. A number of fishermen continued to live in the village, however. Ownership of the harbour was acquired by Brendan Clouston, Baron of Dunure, but it was leased to a local committee, which became Dunure Harbour Committee Association Ltd in 2009. On 10 May 2011 the villagers of Dunure celebrated the 200th anniversary of the creation of the harbour by erecting a plaque in addition to holding various events. In recent years the harbour has appeared in various films, including scenes in *Outlander*, when it doubled as an eighteenth-century Scottish port.

Cuzean Harbour

A gap in the rocks on the shore below Culzean Castle is filled with sand and is known as Culzean Harbour. It was never much of a commercial harbour, but was used regularly in the eighteenth century as a place where the laird could draw up a boat. Long before that, it was probably used as a spot where smugglers brought in their vessels. In 1847 it was noted as a fishing station with twelve boats. On the Ordnance Survey map of 1857, the harbour is delineated, the mouth of it marked by two large poles which were affixed to the rock, and which would indicate the narrow channel between them, where it was safer to draw up a boat. In 1876 the 3rd Marquis of Ailsa established a small shipyard here, known as the Culzean Yacht Building Works. The first vessel to be constructed was the *Beagle*, a racing yacht that was unlucky to be hit by the *Nyanza* in the Kyles of Bute during a race organised by the Royal Clyde Yacht Club. The boat subsequently sank on 2 June 1877, however the crew managed to escape. Other vessels followed, including a fishing punt in 1881, and the yachts, *Cocker* in 1881, the *Finette* in 1882, and the *Snarley Yow* in 1883.

Orders built up, so much so that it was appreciated the site was too small for expansion, and thus a new shipyard was built at Maidens, opening in September 1883. Unfortunately, winter hurricanes twice blew down the large shed at Maidens on top of the machinery, hampering progress. At times of peak demand, the company still used Culzean for additional work. In 1884 the racing yacht *Bedouin* was launched, as was an un-named yacht for T. Troike. A steam launch *Barrdog* of seven tons and a fishing smack followed. The *Violet*, a steam yacht built for the Duke of Montrose was launched in 1884. By 1894 a boat house had been erected in the lee of the cliff, with a slip leading down on the sands, unfortunately at right angles to the narrow sea inlet. In later years the boathouse was used to store a 12-oar lifeboat, manned by employees on the estate. The lifeboat was used to rescue the crew of the *Carl Martins* which was wrecked on the shore on 27 October 1884.

Maidens Harbour

According to the *Statistical Account* of 1791 there were 'eighteen families doing business on the shore' at Maidens. There was no harbour, and only the hillocks of the Pan Knowes afforded protection from the winds and waves. At Wearyneuk boats could be hauled up the sands. The oldest part of the harbour was constructed in the eighteenth century when locals built stone piers into the bay. About half way along the pier was a crane, used for lifting cargoes from various vessels. In the 1870s a lifeboat station was established here by the Marquis of Ailsa. The harbour was rebuilt and extended from August 1913, the cost being £3,000, shared by the 3rd Marquis of Ailsa and the Fishery Board. The works were carried out by Mr MacMonagle, contractor, Ayr. The scheme included the construction of a new sea wall beyond the old pier point, towards the rocks known as the Maiden Ends. This wall was devised to protect the harbour from the north-west storms. However, a storm in 1912 resulted in six fishing boats being either totally wrecked or damaged. In 1881 the fishermen of Maidens were involved in the rescue of a boat from Girvan. To thank them, the Girvan sailors presented a barometer to the village, which was affixed to the village hall. It bears the inscription: 'Presented to the fishermen at Maidens by a few friends of the rescued, in recognition of the prompt action of Andrew Rae, Thomas Girvan, James Boden, Daniel Rodger and William Sloan, in saving the lives of David McCrindle, Thomas White, and James Garey Jr, the crew of the smack *Jane* of Girvan which foundered off Turnberry on Sunday, 10th Oct. 1881.' The 'Maidens Fishing Boat Disaster' occurred on 12 October 1900 with the loss of four lives – two fathers, John Andrew and Matthew Sloan, and two sons, William Andrew and Matthew Sloan. The vessel, the *Maidens Lass*, sank in seventy feet of water around a mile and a half off the shore at Dipple, on the way to Girvan. The boat was raised on 24 October 1900 by local fishermen. A fund raised over £900 by the beginning of November 1900. On 10 November the body of Matthew Sloan, one of the fishermen, was washed ashore at Turnberry.

Maidens from Harbour Breakwater

Maidens harbour has suffered from silting over its existence. In 1948 the harbour was reconstructed, the silt dredged and the pier rebuilt, using rubble from the demolition of RAF buildings at Turnberry aerodrome. The cost was estimated at approximately £85,000, plus an additional £12,000 worth of dredging. This expense was partially funded by Ayr County Council to the value of £10,000, including funds of £3,238 provided by Maidens Fishermen's Harbour Association from their harbour dues fund. The remainder of the money was to be provided by the Treasury; the scheme having been drawn up by the Scottish Home Department. The plans stalled, and in April 1951 a deputation from the county council visited the Scottish Secretary to find out why the scheme had been held up. Developments continued in 1954-8 when a second breakwater was built to the east of the main pier and the original pier was strengthened. This allowed a fair number of fishing boats to base themselves there, landing their catch of herring, cod and other white fish on the pier. In the 1950s there were around ten boats based in the port, each around 50 feet long. Plans were made by the Scottish Home Department to establish the Maidens as the principal landing place for seine or ring-net fishermen, and as part of the scheme Lord Ailsa passed ownership of the harbour to the Maidens Harbour Association. However, by the mid-1970s the harbour had silted up once more, by which time the fishing boats had relocated to either Troon or Ayr. The harbour was in 2011 redeveloped to have a floating pontoon marina within it, attracting yachts and passing vessels. The image shows the harbour from the shore to the east, with the crane on the pier used to land fish. Beyond the headland, at Port Murray, Alexander MacCredie began building steamers in 1883 and the remains of the slip can still be seen. A large shed was constructed and a number of vessels were built there. A short slip led from the yard down into the rocks to the east of Port Murray. MacCredie later moved to the new Ailsa Shipbuilding yard at Troon, where he continued to manage it.

Girvan Harbour

The mouth of the River Girvan has created a natural harbour that has been used for centuries. It hasn't always been a thriving harbour, however, for in 1655 Thomas Tucker noted that it only had 'some five or sixe fisher-boates and not many more houses'. By 1792 the local minister noted that the 'harbour, far from being now a bad one, is capable of much improvement. In its present natural state, the entrance into the harbour is, at high water, from 9 to 11 feet deep; and were a key to be built, which, it is said, might be done for £2,000 or £3,000, it would be rendered considerably deeper.' The harbour became a popular port for herring-fishing vessels, some east-coast vessels basing themselves here for the season. In 1837 a limited-scale quay was built, allowing improved export of coal and grain. In 1846 437 vessels used the harbour, totalling 17,457 tons. A steamer called weekly. There were 34 fishing boats which employed 90 men. In 1954 there were 28 fishing vessels based in the harbour. In 1860 the railway was extended to the harbour, with rails right to the edge of the water on the northern side, allowing coal, timber and grain to be emptied into the boats. In 1865 the harbour was formally set up under the management and control of eight commissioners, four of whom were appointed by the shipowners and the town council. At the time they expected to obtain a low-interest loan with which to make improvements to the harbour, but this was turned down. Instead, a loan was obtained, underwritten by the Earl of Stair and the Glasgow & South Western Railway Company, allowing work to be completed. By 1881 the amount spent had reached £21,000, which included the erection of a small light-tower on the pier. In 1879-80 350 boats had used the harbour in the winter, and fishing for herring was one of the most profitable trades in the area – nearly £100,000 worth of fish caught in a single season. The improvements at the harbour were in part carried out hoping to attract ferry traffic from Northern Ireland. However, when the railway arrived at Stranraer in 1877, and the ferry crossing from there being considerably shorter, Girvan never managed to claim this trade.

Looking at the Boats in Girvan Harbour

The mouth of the River Girvan has created a natural harbour that has been used for centuries. It hasn't always been a thriving harbour, however, for in 1655 Thomas Tucker noted that it only had 'some five or six fisher-boates and not many more houses'. By 1792 the local minister noted that the 'harbour, far from being now a bad one, is capable of much improvement. In its present natural state, the entrance into the harbour is, at high water, from 9 to 11 feet deep; and were a key to be built, which, it is said, might be done for £2,000 or £3,000, it would be rendered considerably deeper.' The harbour became a popular port for herring-fishing vessels, some east-coast vessels basing themselves here for the season. In 1837 a limited-scale quay was built, allowing improved export of coal and grain. In 1846 437 vessels used the harbour, totalling 17,457 tons. A steamer called weekly. There were 34 fishing boats which employed 90 men. In 1954 there were 28 fishing vessels based in the harbour. In 1860 the railway was extended to the harbour, with rails right to the edge of the water on the northern side, allowing coal, timber and grain to be emptied into the boats. In 1865 the harbour was formally set up under the management and control of eight commissioners, four of whom were appointed by the shipowners and the town council. At the time they expected to obtain a low-interest loan with which to make improvements to the harbour, but this was turned down. Instead, a loan was obtained, underwritten by the Earl of Stair and the Glasgow & South Western Railway Company, allowing work to be completed. By 1881 the amount spent had reached £21,000, which included the erection of a small light-tower on the pier. In 1879-80 350 boats had used the harbour in the winter, and fishing for herring was one of the most profitable trades in the area – nearly £100,000 worth of fish caught in a single season. The improvements at the harbour were in part carried out hoping to attract ferry traffic from Northern Ireland. However, when the railway arrived at Stranraer in 1877, and the ferry crossing from there being considerably shorter, Girvan never managed to claim this trade.

Looking up Girvan Harbour

Alexander Noble & Sons established a boat-building yard on the bend of the river in March 1946, initially building timber fishing vessels before developing into the manufacture of steel hulls and specialised craft. Alexander Noble had previously been trained at James Noble's boat-building yard in Fraserburgh (despite the same surname, there was no family connection). Most of the boats built were to Noble's own designs, the first launch being the *Margaret Stephen*, built for local fisherman Peter Stephen. It remained in service under different names until 1993. The first commercial steel-hulled boat built at the yard was the *Kingfisher* II of 1985. Well over 100 boats have been constructed at the yard. The business continues to operate, mainly carrying out repairs and refits. The company was one of only three firms used to carry out the maintenance of lifeboats. A lifeboat has been based at Girvan since 13 January 1865, initially being an oar-powered 32 feet long boat with a small sail which was launched from the beach. The boat cost £400 and was donated by Alexander Key of Glasgow, who named it *Earl of Carrick*. The lifeboat was renamed the *Sir Hope Topham I* (1882-1887). A small lifeboat house was erected at the harbour at a cost of £190.

Sir Hope Topham II followed (1887-1901), then *James Stevens No. 18* (1901-1931), *Lily Glen* (1931-1952), *Frank and William Oates* (1952-1955), *Robert Lindsay* (1955-1960), *Glencoe-Glasgow* (1960-1961), *St Andrew* (1961-1968 and 1976-1977), *James and Barbara Aitken* (1968-1976), *William and Mary Durham* (1976-1983), *Philip Vaux* (1983-1989), *Amateur Swimming Associations* (1989-1993), *Silvia Burrell* (1992-2017) and the *Elizabeth and Gertrude Allan* (from 2017). In more recent years, Girvan has been the home port to various pleasure yachts. The pontoon was erected in 1992, having 35 berths, ten of which are retained for visitors, and these were reconstructed in 2014. Fishing still takes place, and there are also a couple of boats offering fishing trips and tours to Ailsa Craig. South Ayrshire Council took over the harbour in 1996, now operated by Ayrshire Roads Alliance. The fishmarket was closed in 1996, business transferring to Troon. However, in 1997, £870,000 worth of fish and prawns were landed and shellfish remains a popular catch. By 2009 there were only six fishing boats working out of the harbour.

Carleton Port

Although there is no harbour, nor even a pier, at Carleton Port, the beach to the south-west of Lendalfoot had been used by fishing boats for many years. The vessels were drawn up on to the sandy beach, a narrow stretch located between two beds of rock being ideal for the purpose, and the unnamed headland protected the boats from the south west. Houses for fishermen were erected on the raised beach at the head of the port, and these were known as Carleton Fishery. According to the *Edinburgh Evening Courant* of 17 November 1832, 'this is a new and very important establishment ... for introducing there the mode of fishing and curing white fish, which is practised with so much success in the Moray Frith'. The scheme was organised by Mr Johnston, banker in Girvan, and the plan was encouraged by the landowner, Sir John A. Cathcart. The fishermen employed in the scheme were brought from Sandend in Banffshire, 'and being able, experienced, and industrious men, and provided with boats and fishing-tackle of the best description, there can be no doubt of their success on a coast which abounds with all kinds of white fish.' Some of the fishing vessels were also brought from Banffshire, including one which had been built at Cullen, and which won the Loch Ryan Regatta in 1836. The lack of a harbour often resulted in difficulties, and on Monday 18 March 1907 a fisherman named John McCreath was drowned when his small boat overturned in a storm. Four of his companions on the boat had a narrow escape. They had set out in a small vessel to bale out two fishing boats that lay in the bay. After completing the task, their boat was overturned on the way back. McCreath drowned, and three of his associates had to cling to the upturned boat, which they managed to right, before returning to the shore. One of the fishermen was able to swim ashore. The difficulty in landing boats and the increase in their size meant that they were eventually transferred to Girvan. In 1937 there were plans to create a large holiday resort here, including concrete chalets, hotel, cinema, concert hall and golf course, but it was hampered by the war.

Ballantrae Harbour

Work to improve the harbour at Ballantrae commenced in 1847 with a grant of £4,000 from the Fishery Board, the only Ayrshire grant made by the organisation, with the local fishermen contributing £2,000. It was designed by Joseph Mitchell. Around twenty men were employed in the excavation of the basin in May that year, with more men expected to join them. The Royal Commission on Harbours recommended that Ballantrae be developed as a fishery refuge harbour for the southern part of the Carrick coast, but nothing came of this. Complaints were still being made regarding the condition of the harbour in 1850. It was noted that 'for want of a breakwater at the upper end of the main pier, an immense accumulation of sand is constantly taking place. Though specified in the plan, little or no excavation has taken place in the outer end, so that a boat from Girvan grounded there at half tide – became a total wreck – and the crew lost their all, £20 to £30, with materials.' In 1855 Rigby Wason of Corwar proposed to the Lord Lieutenant of Ireland that Ballantrae should be selected as the preferred Scottish port for passage to Ireland, it being closer than Cairnryan or Girvan, and had the advantage of being independent of the government. The harbour at Ballantrae was rebuilt in the late nineteenth century at a cost of £6,000. At this time the pier was rebuilt on a rocky ledge, and in its lee the basin was deepened from the solid rock. For a period the harbour was busy with boats landing white herring. In 1890 1,322 barrels of herring were cured at the port. There were 516 boats involved in landing these, operated by 921 fishermen and boys. On shore the village had 78 fish-curers and 50 men employed in making barrels. In 1890 it was reckoned that the total value of the boats, nets, and other equipment used for fishing was £16,975. Ballantrae was the centre of the South Western Fishery District. The village gives its name to the district for fishing boat registrations – BA. The fishing boats working out of Ballantrae have varied over the years. In 1896 the principal vessels were Zulus, but of a smaller size than normal, being only around 24 to 26 feet in length. When the boats came in, they were landed on the beach and then drawn up over the sands by the aid of a steam winch, for which the men paid around £2 per annum per boat.

Ballantrae Foreshore

Vessels attempting to land at Ballantrae regularly grounded – the list being almost endless. The *Ossian* became stranded on the rocks on 22 December 1887; the *Jessie Paterson* of Irvine was driven onto the rocks at Ballantrae harbour on 27 November 1859 where she bilged, took fire and was burned to the water's edge; on 29 April 1882 a screw lighter from Greenock with coals became stranded at the harbour, the hull half full of water; the *Marion Dick* of Greenock was stranded in December 1894; the *Fawn* of Greenock ran ashore in March 1885 and was making water; the sloop *Trial*, captain Robinson, of Shields, attempted to enter the harbour on 20 March 1877 and ran aground, filled with water and the sea breaking over her; the schooner *Problem* struck a rock at the end of the pier on 7 April 1880, receiving a hole in the hull. In February 1881 John MacSeyney, a fisherman from Girvan, fell from the pier into the harbour and despite managing to grasp a rope that was thrown to him, he fell back into the water and was drowned. The harbour was damaged in a storm in 1885 at a time when 400 boats were based there. In 1890s North British Railways proposed creating a railway line into Ballantrae, with associated pier, envisaging steamers to Larne. The plans did not come to fruition. In 1872 there was a lifeboat based at Ballantrae, little more than a rowing boat, but it was to prove useful in the following years. This view of Ballantrae Foreshore is taken looking north, with Ailsa Craig rising behind the breakwater. The shingle beach was often used for hauling up boats, and a variety can be seen in this view, which dates from around 1910. The row of cottages on the left were erected in the early nineteenth century by the Girvan Building Society to replace older cottages used by the fishermen and their families. In 1936 five boats based in the harbour commenced clam fishing. By 1950 the harbour had lost most of its fishing industry, the *Statistical Account* stating that 'there are only two boats, belonging to an old fishing family, which still make good catches of mackerel, herring and lobsters.'

Acknowledgments

The author would like to thank a few people who have assisted in bringing this book to fruition. In some cases, information was supplied (often years ago!) and in other cases images were supplied. In particular, thanks are due to Tom Dark, Edinburgh University; David Kennedy, The Most Hon. The Marquess of Ailsa; Chris Hawksworth; John Maxwell; the late Margaret Morrell; John Riddell; Craig Sommerville (Girvan RNLI Lifeboat Press Officer); and Alastair Weir.

I would also like to thank the many other people who have supplied information to me over the years, or else pointed me in the right direction for this, the resultant notes and references being filed away just in case they are used in a book at some time in the future.